ANIMALS THAT LIVE ON THE FARM

Sheep

JoAnn Early Macken

Reading consultant: Susan Nations, M.Ed.,
author/literacy coach/consultant

WEEKLY WR READER
EARLY LEARNING LIBRARY

Please visit our web site at: www.earlyliteracy.cc
For a free color catalog describing Weekly Reader® Early Learning Library's list
of high-quality books, call 1-877-445-5824 (USA) or 1-800-387-3178 (Canada).
Weekly Reader® Early Learning Library's fax: (414) 336-0164.

Library of Congress Cataloging-in-Publication Data

Macken, JoAnn Early, 1953–
    Sheep / JoAnn Early Macken.
        p. cm. — (Animals that live on the farm)
    Includes bibliographical references and index.
    ISBN 0-8368-4276-6 (lib. bdg.)
    ISBN 0-8368-4283-9 (softcover)
    1. Sheep—Juvenile literature. I. Title. II. Series.
SF375.2.M33   2004
636.3—dc22
                            2004045129

This edition first published in 2005 by
Weekly Reader® Early Learning Library
330 West Olive Street, Suite 100
Milwaukee, WI 53212 USA

Copyright © 2005 by Weekly Reader® Early Learning Library

Picture research: Diane Laska-Swanke
Art direction: Tammy West
Cover design and page layout: Kami Koenig

Photo credits: Cover, pp. 13, 15, 21 Gregg Andersen; pp. 5, 11 © Daniel Johnson;
p. 7 © Norvia Behling; p. 9 © Alan & Sandy Carey; p. 17 © James P. Rowan;
p. 19 © Adams/Hansen Photography

Printed in the United States of America

1 2 3 4 5 6 7 8 9 08 07 06 05 04

Note to Educators and Parents

Reading is such an exciting adventure for young children! They are beginning to integrate their oral language skills with written language. To encourage children along the path to early literacy, books must be colorful, engaging, and interesting; they should invite the young reader to explore both the print and the pictures.

Animals That Live on the Farm is a new series designed to help children read about the behavior and life cycles of farm animals. Each book describes a different type of animal and explains why and how it is raised.

Each book is specially designed to support the young reader in the reading process. The familiar topics are appealing to young children and invite them to read — and re-read — again and again. The full-color photographs and enhanced text further support the student during the reading process.

In addition to serving as wonderful picture books in schools, libraries, homes, and other places where children learn to love reading, these books are specifically intended to be read within an instructional guided reading group. This small group setting allows beginning readers to work with a fluent adult model as they make meaning from the text. After children develop fluency with the text and content, the book can be read independently. Children and adults alike will find these books supportive, engaging, and fun!

— Susan Nations, M.Ed., author, literacy coach,
and consultant in literacy development

A **lamb** is a baby sheep. Lambs run, jump, and play.

Lambs drink milk from their mothers. Later, they can live on grass.

A **ewe** is a female sheep. A ewe knows its lamb by the smell.

In summer, sheep can stay outside. A group of sheep is called a **flock**.

In winter, sheep may stay in a shed or a barn. The farmer feeds them hay or grain.

Not all sheep are white. Some sheep are black, brown, or gray.

15

Sheep have thick wool coats. A sheep's coat is called its **fleece**. It never stops growing.

Some farmers raise sheep for meat. Some farmers raise sheep for their wool. These sheep are having their fleece **sheared**, or cut.

Some farmers raise sheep for their milk. Have you ever seen sheep on a farm?

Glossary

grain — seeds or fruit from grass plants

hay — grass that is cut and dried for food

sheared — cut

shed — a small building used for shelter or storage

For More Information

Books

From Sheep to Sweater. Start to Finish (series). Robin Nelson (Lerner)

Hooray for Sheep Farming! Bobbie Kalman (Crabtree)

Sheep. Farm Animals (series). Rachael Bell (Heinemann)

Sheep on the Farm. On the Farm (series). Mari C. Schuh (Capstone)

Web Sites

Spring Lambs
www.cyberspaceag.com/visitafarm/photoessays/springlambs/default.htm
Pictures of sheep and lambs

Index

About the Author

JoAnn Early Macken is the author of two rhyming picture books, *Sing-Along Song* and *Cats on Judy*, and four other series of nonfiction books for beginning readers. Her poems have appeared in several children's magazines. A graduate of the M.F.A. in Writing for Children and Young Adults program at Vermont College, she lives in Wisconsin with her husband and their two sons. Visit her Web site at www.joannmacken.com.